DISNEY·PIXAR
MONSTERS, INC.
ESSENTIAL GUIDE

WATERNOOSE

CELIA

ROZ

RANDALL

BOO

DISNEY·PIXAR
MONSTERS, INC.
ESSENTIAL GUIDE

SULLEY

MIKE

Contents

MONSTER MEMO 06

SULLEY 08

MIKE 10

BOO 12

WATERNOOSE 16

RANDALL 18

ROZ 20

CELIA 22

SCARERS 26

SCARE ASSISTANTS 28

WRANGLERS 29

SCARE FLOOR 32

DOOR STATION 34

SIMULATOR ROOM 36

THE C.D.A. 38

BOO'S ROOM 42

THE APARTMENT 44

MONSTROPOLIS 46

ACKNOWLEDGMENTS 48

Monster memo

Disney·PIXAR

MONSTERS, INC.

Fellow Monsters,

Welcome to the world of Monsters, Inc. Let me introduce myself. I am Henry J. Waternoose, the company's Chief Executive Officer.

This corporation has been producing power for over a hundred years, and we are proud of our reputation as the number one scream-collecting firm in Monstropolis.

Throughout the pages of this guide you will meet some of this company's most valuable workers, such as James P. Sullivan, Randall Boggs, and Michael Wazowski. They will show you that we here at Monsters, Inc. are committed to overcoming the current energy crisis.

And might I take this chance to calm any fears about child contamination. We are making every effort to ensure this will never happen at our corporation!

We hope you enjoy this guide to Monsters, Inc. Thank you for spending time with us.

Sincerely,

Henry J. Waternoose

Henry J. Waternoose
President & CEO, Monsters, Inc.

Sulley

Meet James P. Sullivan, or Sulley. He's Monsters, Inc.'s best Scarer. It's his job to frighten children and collect their screams—and he's terrifyingly good at it. In his career with the company, he's quickly soared up the scream-collecting charts. Now Sulley's set to smash the all-time record, which has been held by Fangs McDonald since 1963.

Sulley inherited his blue and purple fur from his mother, and his horns from his father.

Toxic Substance

As any well-informed monster knows, children are highly toxic! So Monsters, Inc. gives its employees careful training on how to deal with children and their belongings. As a result, no child has ever crossed over into the monster world. When Sulley accidentally lets a child through the closet door onto the Scare Floor, he is horrified. Not only could this ruin his career, but the little girl could be very dangerous!

Sulley is 7' 6" tall and weighs 1,460 pounds

SULLEY PROFILE

- Sulley showed a natural talent for scaring at an early age, and his reputation at school aroused the interest of the Monsters, Inc. recruiters.

- His extremely high entrance exam scores in the M.I. Scare Simulator earned him a trainee Scarer position. Within two years he was promoted, and became a full-fledged Scarer.

- After a hard day of scaring at Monsters, Inc., Sulley likes to kick back and relax with an intense physical scare workout.

Big chest for powerful roars

Best Friends

Sulley soon grows to like the child he calls Boo. He is very protective of her, and the pair quickly become friends. This makes Sulley wonder if children really are dangerous after all.

Huge arms and claws—ideal for scaring

Mike and Sulley first met at kindergarten, when Sulley sat on Mike, thinking he was a footstool! Today, they are best friends—as well as the top scaring team at Monsters, Inc.

Mike

Mike Wazowski is a feisty, fast-talking, one-eyed, green ball of a monster. He is Sulley's scare assistant, and no one loves the business of scaring more than Mike. Together, he and Sulley make a great team, and Mike is proud of their scare record. Mike's also pretty fond of the many perks that come with working and living with the top Scarer at Monsters, Inc.

Four-fingered hands

Rubbery froglike skin

An Eyeful

He may have a huge eye, but Mike has not been blessed with good eyesight. As a result, he has to wear a contact lens the size of a soup bowl! He's very picky, so he wouldn't dream of getting his lenses from anywhere other than Cyclops Optical in downtown Monstropolis.

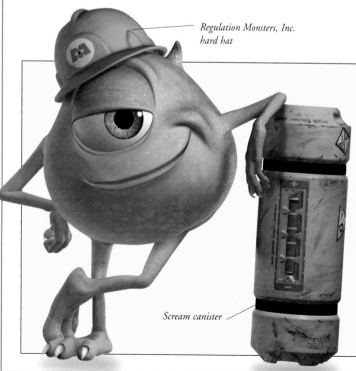

Regulation Monsters, Inc. hard hat

Scream canister

MIKE PROFILE

● Mike processes over 5,000 kid folders a week and over 30 scream canisters per hour at Monsters, Inc. He is Sulley's colleague, roommate, pal, and coach. With a vast knowledge of scaring techniques, Mike helps Sulley prepare for every scaring situation. But he still has trouble filing his paperwork.

● Mike's greatest love is Celia Mae. She's the receptionist at Monsters, Inc. Their favorite date is going to a monster truck rally.

● After a hard week's work at Monsters, Inc., Mike likes nothing better than to put the top down on his car and go for a drive.

Boo thinks that Mike is very funny. She doesn't find his big eye and mini horns frightening at all.

Mini horns

Safety First

Boo throws Mike's life into a tailspin. He spends most of his time trying to protect himself from the toxic child, and trying to come up with a plan to get rid of her for good. His suggestions include: floating her away in a hot-air balloon, firing her into the air with a giant slingshot, and using spoons to dig a tunnel to get her out of the city.

Skinny legs

Monster grin

As Sulley's scare assistant, Mike must keep the furry guy in top scaring shape. Every morning he takes Sulley through his exercises—push-ups, chin-ups, fear squats, and roar lunges.

Little Mikey

He might not be proud of it, but Mike has his own teddy bear. He loves Little Mikey and won't let anyone else touch his toy, so he's horrified when Sulley hands Little Mikey to Boo. Mike snatches the bear back—but hastily returns it when Boo bursts into tears.

Boo

Boo is the energetic little girl who crosses into the monster world and creates chaos there. She immediately takes a liking to Sulley, whom she calls "Kitty," and his best friend, Mike. Boo sees her time in the monster world as one big adventure, and has no idea that she's in danger. Mike and Sulley want to get her home quickly, but Boo is not in any hurry. She's having way too much fun where she is!

Hair in pigtails

One Scared Kitty

Sulley is terrified when he first comes across Boo— after all, kids are toxic! But Boo isn't scared of the giant blue and purple furry creature. To her, he's just one big kitty.

Oversized t-shirt

Girl Of Few Words

Boo doesn't know many words. But Mike and Sulley can usually tell how she is feeling by the look on her face, her tears, or her laughter. When she laughs, the lights in Sulley's apartment glow brighter. Mike and Sulley are surprised and confused by the power produced by her laughter.

Owie

BOO PROFILE

- Boo's real name is Mary Gibbs. Sulley calls her Boo because that is one of her favorite words.

- Boo loves to draw. She draws the monsters that she meets in the monster world. She especially likes to sketch Sulley.

  - At first, Boo is terrified by the nasty monster Randall. But after her adventures with Sulley and Mike in Monstropolis, she becomes less afraid of the slimy, cunning lizard.

    - Boo's favorite game is hide-and-seek. Sulley is amazed by how good she is at hiding.

Mike and Sulley quickly discover that their apartment isn't kid-proof as Boo runs around causing havoc. The monsters try to keep her busy by giving her crayons to draw with and cereal to eat.

Eyes made from Mike's desk lamps

Hair made from an old mop

Cardboard teeth

Flippers and feet made from a bath mat

Body and head made from Sulley's chair

Monster Disguise

...lley finally comes up with a plan
...o get Boo back to her own
...edroom—but it means taking her
...ack to Monsters, Inc. To do this, Sulley
...nd Mike must disguise Boo. So they dress
...er as a monster, using things they find
...round their apartment. The costume fools
...any at Monsters, Inc., but it doesn't stop
...he three of them from getting into trouble.
...oo takes off to explore the city of
Monstropolis, with Mike, Sulley, Randall, and the C.D.A. hot on her heels.

CIRCUS

HORSE

BILLY

Waternoose

Henry J. Waternoose is the CEO, or boss, of Monsters, Inc. This large, crablike monster is the third generation of Waternooses to run the company, and he is determined to see it through the current energy crisis... so determined, in fact, that he would do absolutely anything to keep his company afloat.

Seven-fingered claws

Waternoose is fond of his company's top Scarer—Sulley. He shows a fatherly pride in whatever Sulley does, and even takes an interest when the Scarer brings his cousin's sister's daughter to work—unaware that it's Boo in disguise!

Unwelcome Guests

If there's one thing Waternoose can't stand, it's the Child Detection Agency (C.D.A.). It drives him crazy when they stick their yellow noses into his work. If there is the slightest hint of a child at Monsters, Inc., the C.D.A. will swoop in, stop all scream production, and swamp Waternoose with enough paperwork to drown a crab!

Public Face

As CEO, Waternoose is committed to providing Monstropolis with clean, dependable energy. As he likes to say, "We scare because we care."

Six crab-like legs

Grandfatherly jowls

Waternoose used to be a well-respected Scarer—he virtually wrote the book on training Scarers. One of his best known moves is the "Ol' Waternoose Jump and Growl." It's Sulley's personal favorite.

Clothing befitting a captain of industry

WATERNOOSE PROFILE

• At the tender age of 142, Waternoose took over Monsters, Inc. from his father and transformed it into the modern energy giant that it is today.

• Waternoose is a long-standing member of the Medusa Lodge Local Chapter #242, where he has served two terms as the Grand King Cobra.

• As a boy, Waternoose was educated at a top poison ivy league school. There he was the Captain of the Scare Squad. This was the perfect preparation for a future career in scream collection.

Randall

H e's sneaky, he's sly, he's creepy, he's underhand, and he'll do anything to become the top Scarer at Monsters, Inc. Randall Boggs is a calculating, lizard-shaped monster with eight arms and legs and a mouthful of sharp teeth. He is in direct competition with Sulley to break the all-time scare record, and he is confident that he will succeed. He can't wait to knock Sulley from the top Scarer spot.

Frightening frond

Shifty eye

Walks on legs, slith on eight

Scary Monster

Randall is an exact match for everything that Boo finds scary. That is why he's been specially chosen by the Monsters, Inc. Research and Development department to collect her screams.

RANDALL PROFILE

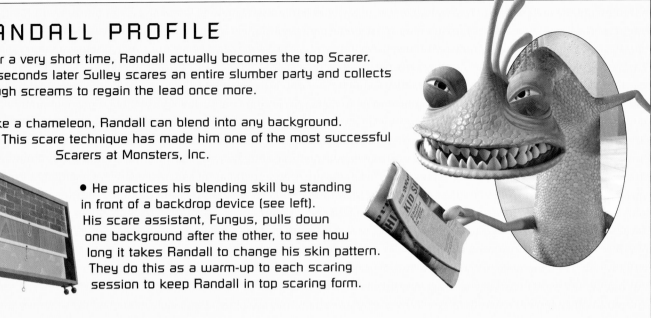

- For a very short time, Randall actually becomes the top Scarer. But seconds later Sulley scares an entire slumber party and collects enough screams to regain the lead once more.

- Like a chameleon, Randall can blend into any background. This scare technique has made him one of the most successful Scarers at Monsters, Inc.

- He practices his blending skill by standing in front of a backdrop device (see left). His scare assistant, Fungus, pulls down one background after the other, to see how long it takes Randall to change his skin pattern. They do this as a warm-up to each scaring session to keep Randall in top scaring form.

Scream Machine

Randall invents a device to extract screams directly from children. All he has to do is kidnap a child and strap him or her into the machine. It then sucks the screams straight into canisters. This means Randall is able to collect lots more screams in one day than he would by traditional scaring. When Randall mistakenly captures Mike instead of Boo, it's the little green guy who gets a taste of the device first. Luckily, the machine is turned off before things go too far!

...ndall's scream machine could collect ...e same number of screams in one ...y as the whole Scare Floor does in ...e month. That means gathering ...gether a lot of scream canisters. ...ndall hides these in his secret lair.

Whiplike tail

Chameleon scales

Roz

Roz loves paperwork and following the correct procedures. She may be slow-moving and slow-talking, but beware any scare assistant who crosses her slimy, sticky path and doesn't file his scare reports correctly— especially a certain Mike Wazowski.

Some example
Roz's paperwo

Soft and cozy
sweater

Sluglike body

Don't Mess With Roz!

As the dispatcher at Monsters, Inc., Roz makes sure that the Scarers are given the right kids to scare. Without her there would be chaos. But it seems that there is something more to Roz's job than meets the eye!

ROZ PROFILE

• Workers at Monsters, Inc. don't know if Roz really needs her horn-rimmed glasses—she always seems to spot any trouble before it starts!

• Forty years ago, Roz was first runner-up in the Miss Monstropolis beauty contest.

• Her guilty pleasure is reading the trashy newspaper *The Daily Glob* during her lunch hour at work.

• As she controls all the paperwork, Roz knows everything about Monsters, Inc. Perhaps even more than she should?

Dispatch Office Hours:

Monday
8:00 a.m. - 2:00 p.m. CMT
Tuesday
6:00 a.m. - 12:00 p.m. CMT
3:00 p.m. - 4:30 p.m. CMT
Wednesday
6:00 a.m. - 12:00 p.m. CMT
3:00 p.m. - 4:30 p.m. CMT
Thursday
4:00 a.m. - 9:00 a.m. CMT
1:00 p.m. - 1:30 p.m. CMT
5:00 p.m. - 8:00 p.m. CMT
Friday
You wish I was in.

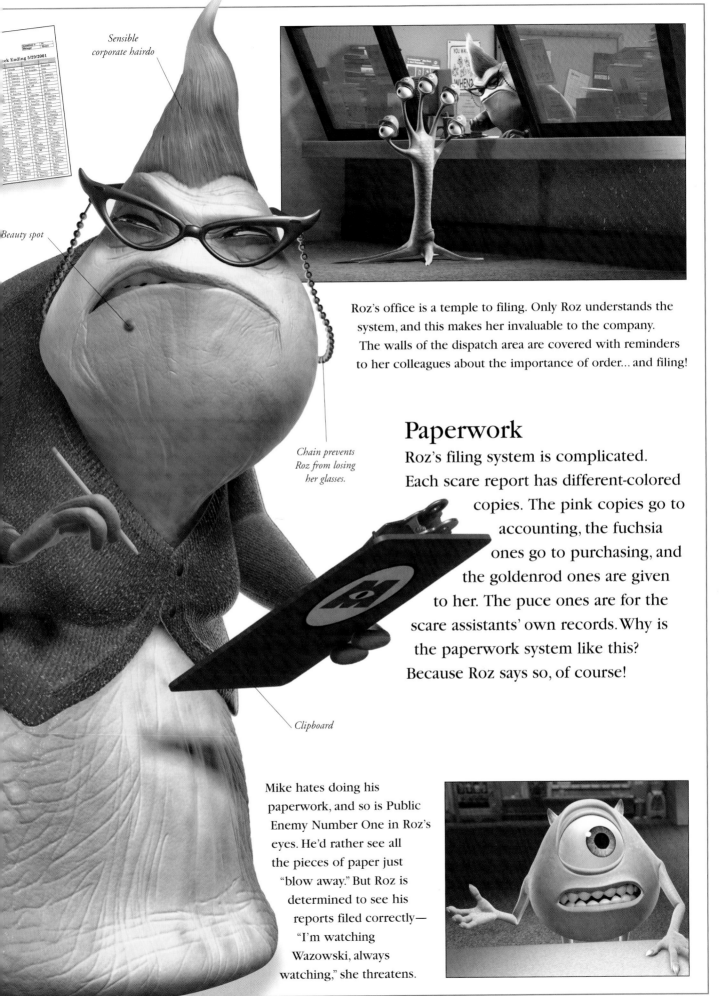

Sensible corporate hairdo

Beauty spot

Chain prevents Roz from losing her glasses.

Clipboard

Roz's office is a temple to filing. Only Roz understands the system, and this makes her invaluable to the company. The walls of the dispatch area are covered with reminders to her colleagues about the importance of order... and filing!

Paperwork

Roz's filing system is complicated. Each scare report has different-colored copies. The pink copies go to accounting, the fuchsia ones go to purchasing, and the goldenrod ones are given to her. The puce ones are for the scare assistants' own records. Why is the paperwork system like this? Because Roz says so, of course!

Mike hates doing his paperwork, and so is Public Enemy Number One in Roz's eyes. He'd rather see all the pieces of paper just "blow away." But Roz is determined to see his reports filed correctly— "I'm watching Wazowski, always watching," she threatens.

Celia

Celia Mae is the receptionist at Monsters, Inc. She is sweet, beautiful, and quite bewitching, particularly to Mike. Things between Mike and Celia are getting pretty serious, until Boo arrives and wreaks havoc. Celia is angry about all the confusion at first, but she still helps Mike and Sulley out when the situation with Randall starts to get tough.

Snake Eyes

Celia's hair is actually made up of five snakes which match her moods—when she's happy, they're happy. When she's sad, so are they. Celia's snakes even have their own names—Amelia, Ophelia, Octelia, Bobelia... and Madge!

Snake hair

*Real f
Celia's*

*Sequin
monster scales*

Tentacles for

Celia Mae is a classic monster beauty. But sometimes even she wants a new look. When she thinks about getting her hair cut, her snakes shake with fear. But Mike likes her hair long, so Celia decides not to go through with it. Phew!

Love Interest

Mike is the lucky monster who gets to date Celia. The two are very much in love. They have silly pet names for each other, like "Shmoopsie-Poo" and "Googly Bear." Despite the trials that life seems to throw at them (namely Boo), Mike is determined to make his relationship work. As he admits to Sulley, "Ya know, pal, she's the one."

Slight Setback

Mike and Celia's love life starts to hit trouble when Mike takes his lovely girlfriend to the super-trendy Harryhausen's Sushi restaurant. Boo's presence causes chaos, the C.D.A. arrives, and Celia ends up being decontaminated by them. That was the worst night of her life, and when she goes to work the next day, she immediately tries to find Mike to get to the bottom of his strange behavior.

CELIA PROFILE

• As the receptionist at Monsters, Inc., Celia is the public face of the company and the first point of contact. She knows everyone's extension by heart, and can answer 10 phone lines without blinking her one eyelid.

• Celia takes a day off each spring so her snakes can shed their skin. Talk about dandruff!

• She may have tentacles for legs, but Celia can still run very fast. She and Mike won the seven-legged race at last year's company picnic.

• In the end, Celia forgives Mike for his shortcomings. After all, they are meant for each other.

Celia at the reception desk

MONSTE

IT'S [IN] THE CAN!

... have developed one

... most sophisticated wa...

... screams, using our patented c...

... d. With the help of the latest c...

... we can match each child w...

... carer to maximise scream...

+ FIZT ∿ v/t   a/e

Once collected, the scream is

sealed in leak-proof cani...

... ped to our pro...

... nt. Here, highly dev...

... tion processes ensu...

... released is pure, un...

... safe for you to us...

When considerin...

... plier, think of Monsters, I...

... your energy needs are in safe hands!

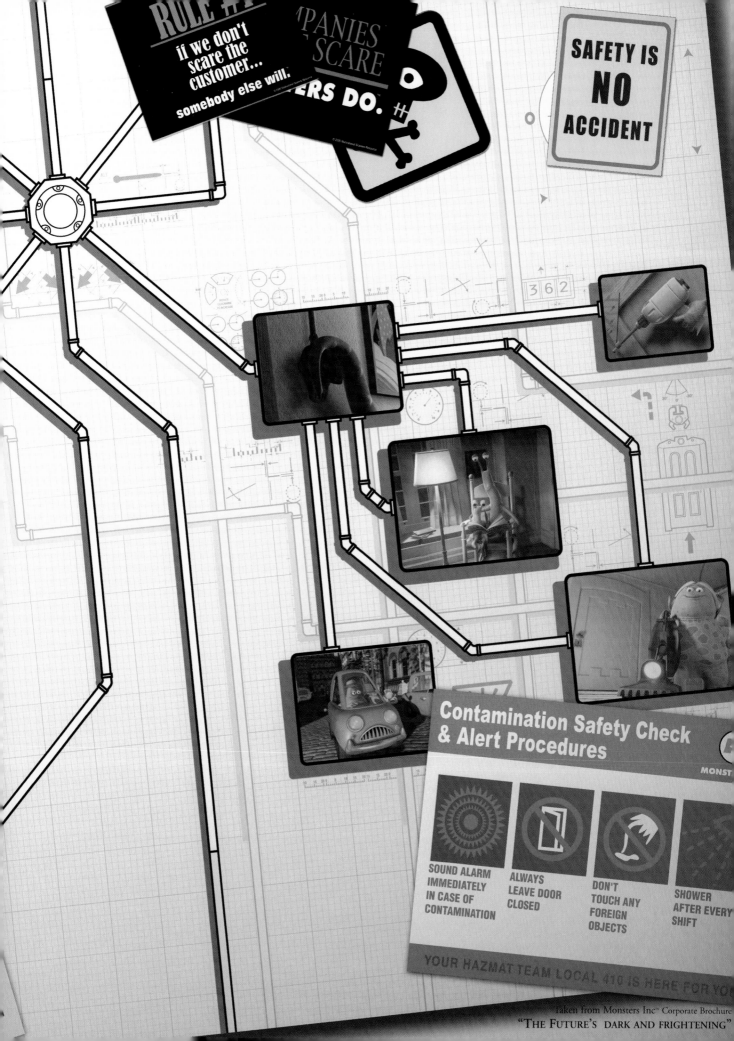

RULE #1
if we don't scare the customer... somebody else will.

...PANIES ...SCARE ...ERS DO.

SAFETY IS NO ACCIDENT

3 6 2

Contamination Safety Check & Alert Procedures

MONST

SOUND ALARM IMMEDIATELY IN CASE OF CONTAMINATION

ALWAYS LEAVE DOOR CLOSED

DON'T TOUCH ANY FOREIGN OBJECTS

SHOWER AFTER EVERY SHIFT

YOUR HAZMAT TEAM LOCAL 410 IS HERE FOR YO

Taken from Monsters Inc™ Corporate Brochure
"THE FUTURE'S DARK AND FRIGHTENING"

Scarers

Scarers are the top workers at Monsters, Inc. They cross over into kids' rooms, despite great danger and huge risk. Their mission is to frighten children and collect the screams. These screams power the monster world. It's a tough job, but these monsters are ready for the challenge.

Single horn

Positive scare attitude

George

George isn't blessed with the best of luck. He has been decontaminated three times for a code 2319. This means that he has brought toxic materials from the human world back into the monster world. Poor George gets a shave with every decontamination—luckily his fur always grows back again!

A good team

A Scarer and his scare assistant have to work as a team. The assistant helps the monster make the most of his or her terrifying skills. This means sharpening claws, polishing fangs, and filing horns. With everything taken care of, all the Scarer has to worry about is being scary!

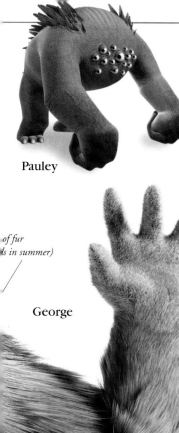

Pauley

Pauley

Strong-but-silent, Pauley is very agile for his size. He likes to sneak up on kids and shock them with his eye-boggling display. Taking care of his eyes isn't cheap—he spends a small fortune on eye drops!

Ricky

*of fur
ds in summer)*

George

Split ends

Ricky takes great pride in his glittering fangs. For some kids, more teeth means more screams.

Bud

It takes a great mix of monsters to match every child's fears. Some kids find Bud's mop of hair very frightening indeed!

Tentacles

Joe

Bob

*Monster
dentures*

THE SCARERS PROFILE

• It's hard to become a Scarer at Monsters, Inc. A rookie has to pass several tough selection tests before he can even begin training. After that, it's many years of hard instruction in simulation rooms and lecture halls. Only once all of these have been completed can a monster truly claim the title of Scarer.

• Every kid monster wants to grow up to be a Scarer.

• A Scarer's job is very stressful. So Scarers have to take three weeks' vacation every year.

Harley

Scare assistants

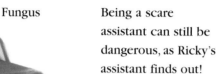

It's not a glamorous job, but scare assistants, like Mike Wazowski, are very important to the scream-collecting process. They take care of the Scarers, and keep them in shape. They visit the dispatch area every day to pick up th scare assignments from Roz, and they also make sure that the Scarers can get back through their doors safely.

Hard hat

Fungus

Three eyes

Being a scare assistant can still be dangerous, as Ricky's assistant finds out!

Fungus

Fungus is Randall's scare assistant. Working alongside such a nasty monster has made Fungus a nervous wreck (although he'd never admit it). Because Fungus is so good at technical things, Randall forces him against his will to build the secret scream extractor.

SCARE ASSISTANT PROFILE

• Some scare assistants are wanna-be Scarers who never made the grade. But others feel that being a scare assistant is their dream job. They love being close to the action, without taking as many of the risks.

• As well as taking care of the Scarers and picking up the scare assignments, a scare assistant has to be on top of his or her paperwork—or else face Roz's anger!

• Assistants need to train for two years before they can work on the Scare Floor.

Wranglers

The lowest entry-level position at Monsters, Inc. is occupied by the wranglers. Their job includes pushing around carts of scream canisters and destroying the doors of kids who aren't scared of monsters anymore.

The Scarers are the scream wranglers' heroes!

The Geeks

Needleman and Smitty are the two wranglers on Mike and Sulley's Scare Floor. And, just like the top scaring team, they have been best friends since childhood.

Needleman

Smitty

Pimpley worm body

Teeth being unstraightened

Scream canister

Skinny body

Today's Lunch

Stick n' Noodle

Pulp...
Macaro...
Beak S...

Invertebra...
Jaundiced...
Fresh M...

SCREAM TEAM LEADER
MONSTERS, INC.
WE SCARE BECAUSE WE CARE

File your
paperwork.

OR ELSE!

MONSTERS, INC.

JAMES P. SULLIVAN

0069-0421-2000
SCARER
SCARE FLOOR F

, INC.

...OWSKI

0061-0210-2000
SCARE ASSISTANT
SCARE FLOOR F

MONSTERS, INC.

M.I. SCARE REPORT

AGE:	4	Race: Caucasian
GENDER:	F	Status: 2

Description:
Energetic, imaginative, artistic, giggler, pron...
to persistant temper tantrums.

History:
Cried at first and subsequent
scares from age 3-4. High capacity
volume. Reevaluate 12-18-01.

Bedwetter:
Y ☐ N ☑

Not...

adjust for F
pitch at +2

AA Grade
Scream

MONSTERS INC.

Room Descritption:
Single closet entry. Door model AA-62, (see
attachment). Single exit to hallway. Window
above bed. Standard entry,low ceiling. Room
kept tidy; minimum clutter hazard. Danger
floor items: Dolls, crayons, plastic pots and
pans, throw rug, lamp cord, jump rope.

Warnings:
Goggles and gloves recommended for safety. Dog acquired 11/71, leve...
2 threat. Parents room nearby: 5 sec. window.

Scheduling:

Logisitics:
Room 13' x 18', single-exit door
hall; single-entry closet (standa...
door frame A6); 8' window seat;
hardwood floor, noise hazard 1.

Second floor room, weight limit
height limit 7'6"; door knob D1...
hinges squeak; no low hanging ha...

2/11 RZ

Scare Schedule fo

Name	Monday
Fungus	Asia
Smith	Asia
Jonas	S. A...
Ray	N...
David	
Nat	
Harley	
Hairb...	
Tia	
Clav...	
Blob	
Spikey	
Randy	
Bile	

MONSTERS, INC.

Scarer of the month

...nes P. Sulliv...

Scare Floor

Welcome to the heart of Monsters, Inc. The Scare Floor is the center of all the company's activities. It's here that the Scarers pass into the human world through kids' closet doors. It is a terrifying journey, with fluffy toys, excitable kids, and angry family pets at every turn. Phew!

This counter shows th number of days since t last case of child contamination.

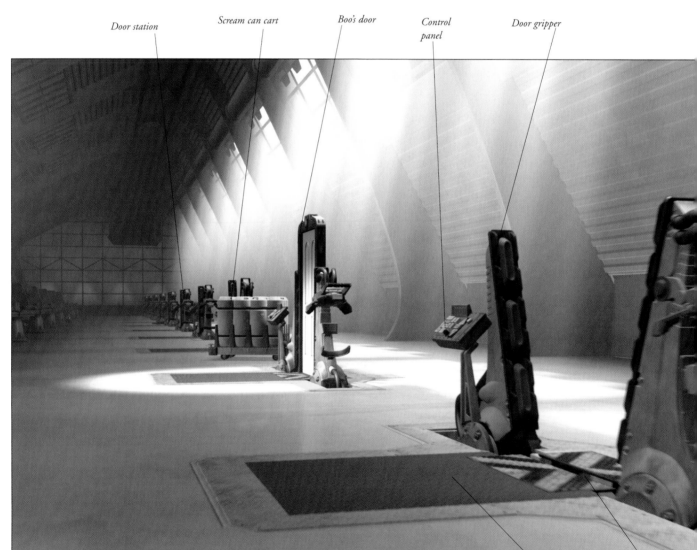

Door station

Scream can cart

Boo's door

Control panel

Door gripper

Footplate

Door l in here

Working On The Scare Floor

During work hours, the Scare Floor is full of activity. Scarers are prepared for scaring and scare assistants shout words of encouragement. Above all the noise, the floor manager counts down the action on his fingers— "We are on in seven... six... five... four...!"

SCARE FLOOR PROFILE

- There are 120 Scare Floors spread over eight floors of the Monsters, Inc. factory.

- Each floor is equipped with 13 door stations – which means that up to 1,560 Scarers can work at any one time!

- When it's busy, the assistants have to dash around removing full scream canisters. These canisters have to be handled with care. The smallest scream leak could cause a massive, uncontrollable power surge!

- One scream canister can hold enough screams to power a monster's house for two days.

Scream canister

Scream canister cart

rganized Chaos

he assistant's workstation
s everything he or she
eds to get a scare team
rough the day. It has a
tion control panel that
orks the lights and a
ecial telephone with a
ceiver that extends to fit
y monster's head.
ost important is the in
d out box carefully
beled "To Be Scared"
d "Scared!"

Reminders to do filing   *Mike's filing system*   *Ignored paperwork*

am leader board   *World map*

Sign Wall

At one end of the Scare Floor is a huge screen. It shows when kids are going to bed in each part of the world. It also displays each Scarer's scream score, and who is in the lead. Randall dreams about being top of this list and beating Sulley to the scream record.

Door station

Monsters, Inc. has relied on the "Closet Door" approach to scaring for over 100 years. Today, the most up-to-date technology is used. Roz decides which kid will be scared. Then a machine carries the door for that room from the door vault to the Scare Floor. The door is locked into a Monsters, Inc. door frame and is powered up. Once it's activated, the monster can begin his scare assignment.

Each door leads into a different kid's bedroom.

Kid's I.D. number

Monsters, Inc. door frame

When the assistant gets his Scarer's assignments, he also gets coded swipe cards – one for each child. This card tells the system which door to call up from the vault.

Card reader

Station controls eject button

Left door gripper

Control panel

Boo's door

Control Panel

There is a control panel attached to every door station. A scare assistant uses it to call up the required door and to check the kid's I.D. number on the display. It is also used to send the door back once the scaring is over.

Door track

Scream hoses

Door claw

Door grabber stowed

Millions of doors are stored in the door vault – one for every kid in the world! These doors are taken to the Scare Floor along miles and miles of track.

Door station mat

DOOR STATION PROFILE

- The door station is a big, complicated piece of machinery which was developed especially for Monsters, Inc.

- Once a door is brought in from the door vault, the door grabber reaches up and grabs the door from the track. The door is then carefully lowered into the door station.

- In the early days, thousands of wranglers used to carry the doors from the door vault by hand (or claw, or tentacle.)

Door activation light

Door grabber

Telescoping pneumatic piston

Scream hoses

High-pressure scream canister cap

Open Sesame!

Each door is delivered to a door station on the Scare Floor. Special clamps hold the door in place and connect it to a scream canister. A red light comes on to show that the door is ready to use. It signals to the Scarer that he can enter the kid's bedroom.

Scream canister gauge

Scream canister

Door gripper hinge

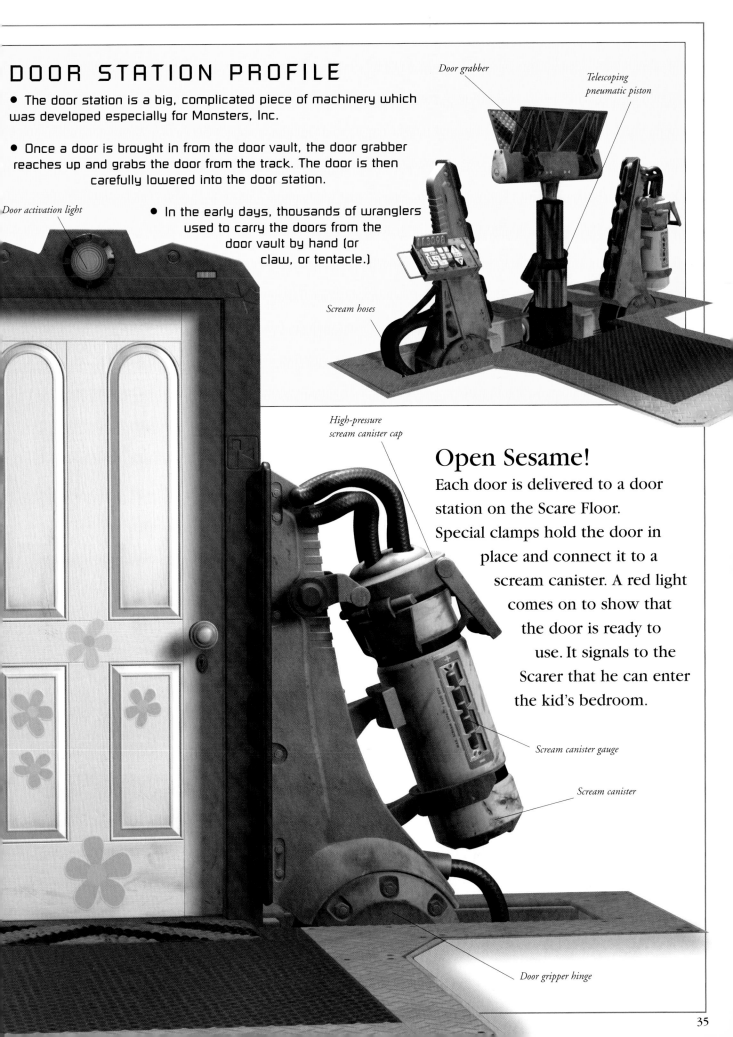

Simulator room

Trainee Scarers practice their scaring skills in the simulat[or] room. Here they learn that there's much more to the job than putting on a scary face. Set up to look like a real child'[s] bedroom, the simulator room gives the recruits a taste of a real scare assigment. It presents them with every danger tha[t] they could meet in the human world—all under the watchful eye of their trainer, Ms. Flint.

Ms. Flint oversees the training of all would-be Scarers.

Today's new recruits are not very good. Despite all Ms. Flint's lessons, they keep getting things wrong. They even touch a kid's toy! These trainee monsters have a lot to learn before they can join the ranks of the Scarers.

A Scary Job

The job of Scarer is the most risky in the scream collection business. Danger lurks around every corner of a kid's bedroom. The Scarers owe it to the other monsters to make sure that a kid doesn't enter their world and pollute it. Plus, a Scarer must never be caught by a child, parent, or pet! So Monsters, Inc. gives its Scarers the very best training that money can buy.

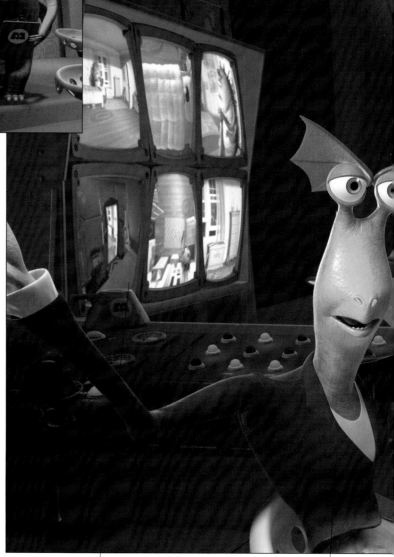

Instant video playback

Ms. Flint

THE SIMULATOR ROOM

- The simulator room has the very best technology to train the budding Scarers in proven scare techniques.

- A lifelike robotic kid is used in place of a human child. It acts exactly as a real child would. Trainees, beware!

- The simulator room is equipped with an instant video playback system. This means that the new recruits can immediately view their scare performance—and all their mistakes are captured on camera for everyone to see!

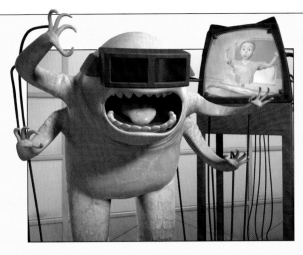

A trainee Scarer uses computer technology to practice his scaring technique.

Simulator Room

Control panel

Practice Makes Perfect

Thaddeus Bile is a trainee Scarer. But he isn't doing too well. Like many first-time Scarers, he is not very experienced. He makes lots of mistakes in the simulator room, including the worst mistake of all—leaving the closet door open!

Bile

The C.D.A.

The C.D.A. uses an armored, hi-tech vehicle to get to contamination emergencies quickly.

Scream power may provide monsters with all of their energy needs, but it's not without its risks—after all, children are toxic. That's where the Child Detection Agency (the C.D.A.) comes in. This squad of highly trained agents are always ready to protect monsters from the dangers of child contamination.

Personal atmosphere purification unit

Multiple eye lenses

0002

Corporate Target

The C.D.A. was called to a kid sighting at Harryhausen's restaurant. While examining the scene, they found a Monsters, Inc. gym bag. This made them very suspicious of the company, and they started to investigate.

Regulating valve

Air intake grill

A C.D.A. agent is fully equipped to deal with any situation. He even carries his own air supply on his back!

Triple-layer protective glo

Hazardous environment suit

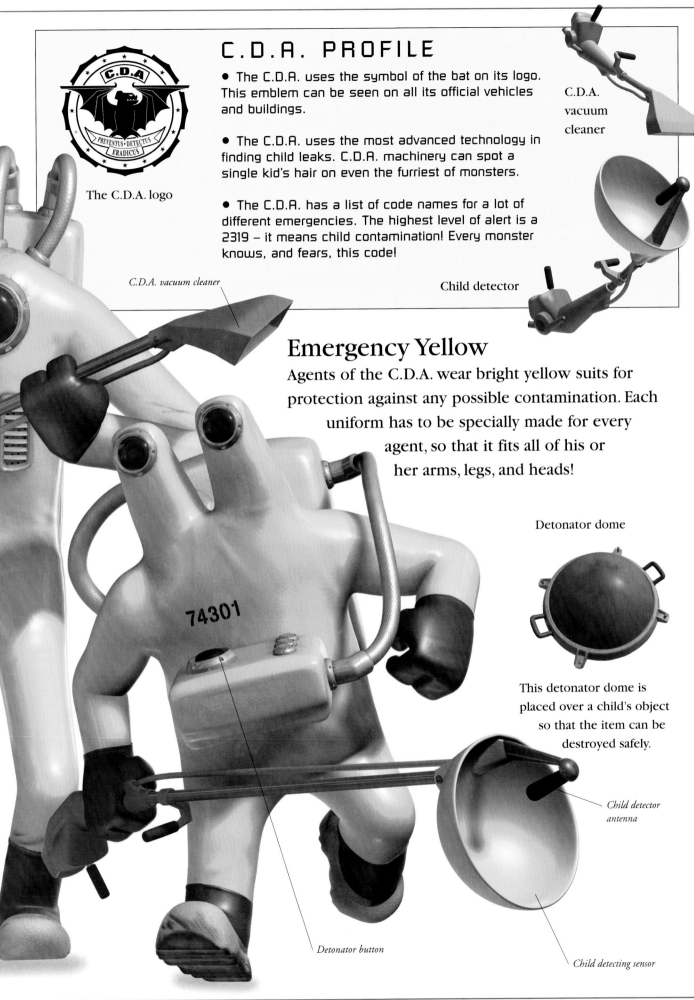

C.D.A. PROFILE

- The C.D.A. uses the symbol of the bat on its logo. This emblem can be seen on all its official vehicles and buildings.

- The C.D.A. uses the most advanced technology in finding child leaks. C.D.A. machinery can spot a single kid's hair on even the furriest of monsters.

- The C.D.A. has a list of code names for a lot of different emergencies. The highest level of alert is a 2319 – it means child contamination! Every monster knows, and fears, this code!

The C.D.A. logo

C.D.A. vacuum cleaner

C.D.A. vacuum cleaner

Child detector

Emergency Yellow

Agents of the C.D.A. wear bright yellow suits for protection against any possible contamination. Each uniform has to be specially made for every agent, so that it fits all of his or her arms, legs, and heads!

Detonator dome

This detonator dome is placed over a child's object so that the item can be destroyed safely.

Child detector antenna

Detonator button

Child detecting sensor

stropolis Horn EXTRA

MONSTOROPOLIS'S LARGEST NEWSPAPER

MONDAY AUGUST 14, 2001

1 SHORTAGE LOOMS

Modern Kids Hard to Scare

LOB

1.693¹/²

MARCH 26, 2001

.I. CEO Waternoose

luminum Plains. ead here is
olored orange before the sunset
of the dawn of civilization.
Meanwhile while most of us are.

INSIDE

"Why we Scare" (A-2)

ridge B-2	Movies B-6
usiness C-1	Obituaries A-21
lassified B-9	Sports D-1
omics B-5	Stocks C-5
rossword B-7	Style B-1
oroscope B-2	Weather A-20

*Having
rouble
etting your
Horn? Call
800) 555
HORN*

54682 30100

BORN

RS INC. PRESENTS
AL JAZZ FESTIVA

Executive Briefcase

$47.991

Office Supply
Savings for the
Entire
Family

S
TS
ED

ter
LD

CENTAUR'S

OPEN EVERY NITE TIL DAWN

Boo's room

The door to Boo's room

O ne night, while catching up on Mike's paperwork, Sulley goes back to the Scare Floor. There he finds a door that has not been put away. Thinking there might be a monster inside, he steps through the door into the room of a little girl. After checking to see if anybody is scaring in there, he leaves. But a small child grabs ahold of his tail and follows him...

Budding Artist

Boo thinks Sulley looks like the big, furry teddy bears and kitty cats that she loves to draw. That's why she follows him through the closet door.

Boo's toy basket

INSIDE BOO'S ROOM

● Boo has everything a little girl could want in her room including a table for tea parties, a four-poster bed and a giraffe growth chart to measure her height.

● Boo's room is a level 2 threat to any scaring monsters. This means that her parents' room is nearby and that the family has a dog.

● Boo has lots and lots of toys at home. She can't wait to show Sulley some of her favorites, like her squeaky fish and her much-loved Jessie doll.

Boo's line of wooden duckies gets tangled up in Sulley's tail and he drags it through to Monsters, Inc.

More of
Boo's toys

Boo's Mom and Dad
bought her this mobile.
It helps her to sleep.
Hanging from it are a cow
jumping over the moon
and a cat playing a fiddle.

Boo's drawings

Boo's
mobile

Boo's bed   *Chair for reading stories*

Playful Girl

Boo likes her toys where she can see them – all over her
bedroom floor! Unfortunately, poor Sulley gets completely
tangled up in them when he stumbles out of her room and
back into Monsters, Inc.

The apartment

Even though Mike and Sulley make a good living working at Monsters, Inc., they still live in the apartment they first moved into after college. It's not in the nicest part of Monstropolis, but their neighbors are friendly and the two monsters are happy there. Plus, it's near work, and there's a great view of the whole city from their window.

No Place Like Home

Mike and Sulley's apartment is a true bachelor pad. The furniture should be replaced, but they like it. They prefer to eat out rather than cook, and their refrigerator usually contains old takeout containers, a jar of pickles, and a moldy piece of cheese. Their mantel is decorated with pictures of the two friends together, including their graduation portrait. Mike also keeps "Little Mikey" on the mantel. This is Mike's special teddy bear. Even though Mike is grown up, he still loves his teddy bear and won't let anyone play with it.

Little Mikey

INSIDE THE APARTMENT

Sulley's favorite armchair

State-of-the-art technology

• Sulley's armchair was bought at a garage sale 10 years ago. The furry monster finds it very comfortable —especially since it has a hole for his tail. But that doesn't stop him from cutting the chair up to make a disguise for Boo.

• As a real music fan, Mike insists on using the best stereo to play his huge collection of CDs. It cost him most of a month's salary—but he thinks that it's worth every penny.

• There are two doors to their apartment —a large one for Sulley, and a smaller one for Mike.

Mike's stereo

Mike's CD stack   *Stereo*

ike and Sulley's apartment sits on the top floor of
onster Towers on the lower east side of
onstropolis. They still live in the same neighborhood
at they grew up in—and they are the local heroes!

iny Terror

o is delighted by Mike and Sulley's
artment and runs wild. She blows
e lights just by laughing, destroys
eir TV, and ruins Mike's carefully
phabetized CD collection. She
nerally makes a nuisance of herself, but
e two monsters are powerless to
op her—they're too scared that she
ight be toxic!

Monstropolis

Monstropolis is the bustling center of the monster world. By day, its streets are abuzz with business. In the evening, the monsters enjoy the city nightlife. Come along to Monstropolis, and see for yourself— unless you're a human kid, of course!

The *Monstropolis Horn* is the city's be selling newspaper.

City by Nigh

When the sun sets, Monstropolis really comes to life In the evening, the monsters can relax and enjoy themselv at the city's many f restaurants, movie theaters, and theate Even the biggest, most fearsome monsters cannot h but have a tentacle tapping good time the city's jazz and dance clubs!

Car Love

Monsters love their cars! Even though many of them don't have hands to steer, this doesn't stop them from driving around the city. But, today everyone is being encouraged to travel by foot, or tentacle, because of the scream shortage. City posters remind everyone to "Conserve scream. Take a walk!"

CITY PROFILE

Mike's convertible

- Monstropolis is growing. The head count last year (including those monsters with more than one head) was over 6.5 million, and rising!

- Monstropolis' proud history can be seen in its rich and unusual building designs. The strong iron and stone work may look beautiful, but these materials are needed to support the weight of the huge, heavy monsters inside!

- The city's public transportation system is the best in the monster world. On the tram network, there are cars of different sizes. This means every monster can travel in comfort—from the biggest to the smallest.

DON'T STALK

Street crossing sign

Newspaper stand

Harryhausen's is one of Monstropolis' best restaurants. Tables must be reserved a month in advance. But the wait is worth it. Its delicious menu includes swill-and-sour soup, spider roll, and blueberry slobber.
The chef is the fastest in town, thanks to his eight arms!

Monster Company

onstropolis has grown up ound one industry—scream oduction. Monsters, Inc. is e city's biggest employer. It s helped to establish the ty library, two fire stations, d most recently, the Henry Waternoose Center for rforming Arts.

"We're MONSTERS, INC!"

LONDON, NEW YORK, MUNICH, PARIS,
MELBOURNE, DELHI

WRITTEN BY Jon Richards
EDITOR Rebecca Knowles
SENIOR DESIGNER John Kelly
DESIGNERS Ellie Healey and Guy Harvey
U.S. EDITORS Gary Werner and Margaret Parrish
DTP DESIGNER Jill Bunyan
PUBLISHING MANAGER Cynthia O'Neill
ART DIRECTOR Cathy Tincknell
PRODUCTION Nicola Torode

First American Edition, 2001

01 02 03 04 05 10 9 8 7 6 5 4 3 2 1

Published in the United States by DK Publishing, Inc., 95 Madison Avenue, New York, NY 10016

Reproduced by M.D.P., UK
Printed and bound by Quebecor World, USA

Acknowledgments

Dorling Kindersley would like to thank:
Lori Heiss, Hunter Heller, Eric Huang, Deirdre Cutter,
Tim Lewis, Graham Barnard, Victoria Saxon, Teri Avanian
and Rachel Alor at Disney Publishing Worldwide;
Pete Docter, David Silverman, Lee Unkrich, John Lasseter,
Darla Anderson, Michele Spane, Leeann Alameda,
Krista Swager,Bob Peterson, Bob Pauley, Katherine Sarafian,
Jonas Rivera, Andrea Warren, Clay Welch, Brian Tindall,
Keith Kolder, Kevin Chang, Kathleen Chanover, and
The Staff at Pixar Animation Studios

Library of Congress Cataloging-in-Publication Data

Richards, Jon, 1970-
    Monsters, Inc. essential guide / by Jon Richards.-- 1st American ed.

      p. cm.
    Summary: An illustrated guide to the characters in the animated film
"Monsters, Inc."
      ISBN 0-7894-7941-9
    1. Monsters, Inc. (Motion picture)--Juvenile literature. [1.
Monsters, Inc. (Motion picture)]   I. Title.
    PN1997.2.M6 R53 2001

    791.43'72--dc21   2001032545

see our complete

catalog at

www.dk.com